FTCE Technology Education 6-12 Exam

"You never fail until you stop trying" - Albert Einstein

For inquiries;
info@xmprep.com

Unauthorised copying of any part of this test is illegal.

FTCE Technology Education 6-12 Exam #1

Test Taking Tips

☐ Take a deep breath and relax

☐ Read directions carefully

☐ Read the questions thoroughly

☐ Make sure you understand what is being asked

☐ Go over all of the choices before you answer

☐ Paraphrase the question

☐ Eliminate the options you know are wrong

☐ Check your work

☐ Think positively and do your best

Table of Contents

SECTION 1 - TECHNOLOGY	
DIRECTION	1
PRACTICE TEST	2 - 11
ANSWER KEY	12
SECTION 2 - EDUCATION	
DIRECTION	13
PRACTICE TEST	14 - 24
ANSWER KEY	25
SECTION 3 - TECHNOLOGY	
DIRECTION	26
PRACTICE TEST	27 - 36
ANSWER KEY	37
SECTION 4 - EDUCATION	
DIRECTION	38
PRACTICE TEST	39 - 51
ANSWER KEY	52
SECTION 5 - TECHNOLOGY	
DIRECTION	53
PRACTICE TEST	54 - 65
ANSWER KEY	66

Copyright © Educational Testing Group, All rights reserved.
This booklet may not be reproduced and transmitted in any form by any means without the permission of the publisher.
This booklet has been prepared and printed in USA.

TEST DIRECTION

DIRECTIONS

Read the questions carefully and then choose the ONE best answer to each question.

Be sure to allocate your time carefully so you are able to complete the entire test within the testing session. You may go back and review your answers at any time.

You may use any available space in your test booklet for scratch work.

Questions in this booklet are not actual test questions but they are the samples for commonly asked questions.

This test aims to cover all topics which may appear on the actual test. However some topics may not be covered.

Studying this booklet will be preparing you for the actual test. It will not guarantee improving your test score but it will help you pass your exam on the first attempt.

Some useful tips for answering multiple choice questions;

- Start with the questions that you can easily answer.

- Underline the keywords in the question.

- Be sure to read all the choices given.

- Watch for keywords such as NOT, always, only, all, never, completely.

- Do not forget to answer every question.

1

Which of the following would be the main concern of community planners prior to the building of a car-manufacturing factory's plans for a new plant?

A) The operating hours of the plant
B) The employee's work environment at the plant
C) The number of materials to be kept in the plant
D) The plant's impact on the environment

2

Which of the following is chiefly responsible for the forward movement of a fixed-wing aircraft?

A) Thrust
B) Lift
C) Weight
D) Drag

3

What does the acronym "OS" stand for?

A) Open software
B) Operating system
C) Optical Sensor
D) Order of significance

4

Which of the following is most commonly used for providing the structural strength of truss bridges?

A) Rectangular units
B) Hexagonal units
C) Circular units
D) Triangular units

CONTINUE ▶

5

Through molecular biology, a revolution in vaccine development has started.

Which of the following innovations in this field has contributed to the most recent changes in vaccine development?

A) Synthesis of vaccines made up of viral coat proteins which trigger immune responses.
B) Production of vaccines containing live pathogenic agents
C) Vaccines that provide lifelong immunity had been created.
D) Manufacturing of vaccines that allow transmission of lifelong immunity from one generation to the following generation.

6

In a vehicle, which system provides the vehicle necessary power for movement?

A) Control
B) Propulsion
C) Guidance
D) Structural

7

A control system is a system which controls other systems.

Which of the following about the control systems is not correct?

A) Auto-pilot for an aircraft is a closed loop system.
B) In an automatic control system sensors are not used.
C) In an open loop system, the control action is independent of the output.
D) In an open loop system, recalibration is not required for maintaining the quality of the output.

8

Environmental Protection Agency is purposely built to ensure for protecting the environment from air and water pollution. Which of the following is the agency also responsible for protecting?

A) Human rights
B) Transportation systems
C) Human health
D) All of the above

9

What is the approximate power dissipation, in watts, of an electrical circuit that consists of a 36V battery and three 6 ohm resistors all connected in series?

A) 2
B) 36
C) 72
D) 216

10

Balloon framing is a style of wood-house building that uses long, vertical 2" x 4"s for the exterior walls.

Platform framing (also known as western framing) is the most common framing method for residential construction where each floor of a pole barn or conventional building is framed independently by nailing the horizontal framing member to the top of the wall studs.

In residential construction, which of the following about balloon framing is not correct?

A) Balloon framing uses shorter pieces of lumber.
B) Balloon framing has an increased wind load strength.
C) Balloon frame structures also have less settling than platform framing as a result of shrinkage.
D) In balloon style, the wall studs ran the entire height of the building, from foundation to attic spaces.

11

When selecting a material to use for the floor of a garage, it is most important to consider resistance to which of the following?

A) Shear; a force that cuts off the materials
B) Tension; a force that streches the materials
C) Torsion; a force that twists the materials
D) Compression; a force that squeezes the materials

12

Which of the following file extensions should be checked when scanning for viruses in a drive?

A) .wav (Audio File Format)
B) .exe (Executable File Format)
C) .pdf (Portable Document Format)
D) .jpg (Joint Photographic Experts Format)

CONTINUE ▶

13

When lead builds up in the body, **lead poisoning** occurs and it can cause serious health problems.

Which of the following in older dwellings can be one of the reasons of lead poisoning?

A) Insulation materials on the walls.
B) Paint on the walls and woodwork.
C) Frayed electrical wirings and switches.
D) Corroded pipes and channels of heating and cooling systems.

14

In a large-scale commercial construction venture, which of the following is normally the first step that needs to be taken?

A) Applying for building permits and variances
B) Holding a discussion with the developer, designer, and contractor regarding the scope of the construction
C) Ordering the necessary materials for building the foundation
D) Drafting a contract specifying details of the building plan

15

What is the primary function of a transformer?

A) To block the electricity flow.
B) To increase, decrease or maintain the voltage amount.
C) To ground an electrical circuit in case of a current surge.
D) To increase the amount of current passing through the wire.

16

Which type of wall provides the support needed to withstand weight from a building's ceiling and roof?

A) Stud-support
B) Rafter-plate
C) Load-bearing
D) Ceiling-joist

17

Presence of water in the hydraulic system in farm machinery can have adverse effects on performance and durability. Which of the following could indicate the presence of water in farm machinery?

A) A grayish, milky fluid
B) A noisy relief valve
C) Excessive thinning of the fluid
D) Excessive fluid use

18

Understanding and knowledge regarding which of the following is crucial in the successful design of graphic communication messages?

A) The limitations of the printer
B) The capabilities of the designer
C) Current technologies
D) The nature of the audience

19

The kilobyte is a multiple of the unit byte for digital information. How many bits are there in a KiloByte?

A) 1000
B) 8192
C) 1024
D) 8024

20

The diesel internal combustion engine differs from the gasoline powered Otto cycle by using highly compressed hot air to ignite the fuel rather than using a spark plug.

Which of the following is not true about the diesel engines?

A) Diesel engines work by compressing only the air.
B) It is also known as a compression-ignition or CI engine.
C) The diesel engine has high thermal efficiency.
D) The fuel and air are usually mixed in the carburetor.

21

Mark intends to build a garage and is determining the materials he needs for the garage's floor. It is important that the material Mark chooses should be resistant to which of the following?

A) Shear
B) Torsion
C) Tension
D) Compression

22

Which of the following about the loop systems is not correct?

A) Another name given to Open-loop system is the Non-feedback system.
B) An Open-loop system, is a type of continuous control system in which the output has no influence or effect on the control action of the input signal.
C) An electric clothes dryer is an example of Closed-loop system because it will automatically stop and turn-off even if the clothes where still wet or damp.
D) A Closed-loop control system is a set of mechanical or electronic devices that automatically regulates a process variable to the desired state or setpoint without human interaction.

23

Fault tolerance is the property that enables a system to continue operating properly in the event of the failure of some of its components.

A plan for ensuring the fault tolerance of a computer network would most likely contain a strategy for which of the following?

A) Increasing the network bandwidth
B) Encrypting the most sensitive data
C) Maintaining uninterrupted power
D) Installing a proxy server on the host

24

It is associated with the processing of comparison speed. It is a method of measuring the raw speed of a computer's processor. Its measurement doesn't take into account other factors such as the computer's I/O speed or processor architecture.

Which of the following is explained above?

A) CPS (Characters Per Second)
B) FFT (Fast Fourier Transform)
C) MIPS (Million Instructions Per Second)
D) MPG (Moving Picture Experts Group)

25

The syntax error is a character or string incorrectly placed in a command or instruction that causes a failure in execution.

Which of the following is a process of testing a program for any syntax or logic errors?

A) Editing
B) Double checking
C) Decoding
D) Debugging

26

Information technology (IT) is the application of computers to store, study, retrieve, transmit, and manipulate data often in the context of a business.

Which of the following summarizes the term "Information Technology"?

A) Computers + Network
B) Hardware + Software
C) Computers + Connectivity
D) Connectivity + Hardware

27

Which of the following would be the primary concern of community planners before building a car-manufacturing factory's plans for a new plant?

A) The operating hours of the plant
B) The employee's work environment at the plant
C) The number of materials to be kept in the plant
D) The plant's impact on the environment

28

Wireless service is a service offering the transmission or receipt of messages by wireless telegraphy or telephony.

Current trends in the field of IT aim at providing wireless services to people while improving the speed and storage space of existing computer systems. The term 'wireless services' means which of the following?

A) Without cables
B) The increase of the memory of the computer
C) Reduction in the size of computers
D) Reduction in cost of computers

29

A reference guide has just been updated. Upon accessing the file, a few employees are confused about which of the printed documents is the latest update.

What feature should be included in the reference guide to avoid this confusion?

A) The names of the authors
B) Version number
C) The copyright information
D) Data printed

30

Computer memory is any physical device capable of storing information temporarily or permanently.

Which of the following gives a list of memory in increasing order (slow to fast) of speed access?

A) L1 Cache, RAM, Hard Disk, L2 Cache
B) Hard Disk, RAM, L2 Cache, L1 Cache
C) L1 Cache, L2 Cache, RAM, Hard Disk
D) RAM, Hard Disk, L1 Cache, L2 Cache

31

An operating system is the most important software that runs on a computer. It manages the computer's memory and processes, as well as all of its software and hardware.

Which of the following is NOT a function of the Operating System?

A) Memory management
B) Database management
C) Process management
D) Disk management

32

Like any other equipment, a computer needs special care and attention in order to perform properly and safely.

Which of the following statement is not included in a "special care" to ensure that data saved on your CD/DVD is preserved?

A) Do not expose your CD/DVD to extreme temperature
B) Clean the CD/DVD with a brush, in an outward direction from the center of the disk, avoiding circular movements, to remove dust
C) Store them in their casing – any scratch makes it difficult to read through the reflective coating
D) Do not write on the reflective coating of the CD/DVD and use only recommended marker for any labeling on the label side

33

The hexadecimal numeral system is a numeral system made up of 16 symbols. The standard numeral system is called decimal and uses ten symbols.

Which of the following is the decimal value of 30 in Hexadecimal?

A) 11010
B) 1E
C) 30
D) 1C

34

CAD, or computer-aided design and drafting (CADD), is the use of computer technology for design and design documentation.

Which one is best suited for use with paper of large size and for complex drawings in Computer Aided Design?

A) Laser printer
B) Dot-Matrix printer
C) Ink-Jet printer
D) Pen Plotter

35

Which of the following is the estimated power dissipation of an electrical circuit comprising a battery with 12 volts that is connected to two 7 ohms resistors in series?

A) 168 watts
B) 1.75 watts
C) 10 watts
D) 20 watts

36

In a manufacturing laboratory, a student asks his teacher what assembly procedures should be used when solving a fabrication problem.

Which of the following would be the teacher's best response?

A) Provide possible assembly procedures for the student to select
B) Ask the student to make their judgment and decide
C) Provide an opinion on the best assembly procedure for the problem
D) Use leading questions to guide the student in analyzing the merits of different assembly procedures

37

Solid-state storage is a type of non-volatile computer storage that stores and retrieves digital information using only electronic circuits, without any involvement of moving mechanical parts.

Which of the following is a characteristic of Solid State Storage devices?

A) They have no moving parts
B) Data cannot be erased from them once written.
C) They have greater storage capacity than Hard disks.
D) They consume a lot of power.

38

A high-level language is a programming language that enables a programmer to write programs that are more or less independent of a particular type of computer while machine language is a set of instructions executed directly by a computer's central processing unit.

In programming, which of the following converts high-level language into machine language?

A) Converters
B) Drivers
C) Translators
D) Service programs

39

The mouse, sometimes called a pointer, is a hand-operated input device used to manipulate objects on a computer screen.

Which of the following types of mouse is a battery-powered device that transmits data using wireless technology such as radio waves or infrared light waves?

A) Cordless Mouse
B) Trackball
C) Optical Mouse
D) Mechanical Mouse

40

BIOS (Basic Input Output System) is the program that a personal computer's microprocessor uses to get the computer system started after you turn it on.

The BIOS is located in which part of the computer?

A) ROM (Read-Only Memory)
B) CMOS (Complementary Metal-Oxide-Semiconductor)
C) MBR (Master Boot Record)
D) RAM (Random Access Memory)

SECTION 1 - TECHNOLOGY

#	Answer	Topic	Subtopic	#	Answer	Topic	Subtopic	#	Answer	Topic	Subtopic	#	Answer	Topic	Subtopic
1	D	TB	S2	11	D	TB	S2	21	D	TB	S2	31	B	TB	S1
2	A	TB	S2	12	B	TB	S1	22	C	TB	S2	32	B	TB	S1
3	B	TB	S1	13	B	TB	S2	23	C	TB	S1	33	B	TB	S1
4	D	TB	S2	14	B	TB	S2	24	C	TB	S1	34	D	TB	S1
5	A	TB	S4	15	B	TB	S3	25	D	TB	S1	35	C	TB	S3
6	B	TB	S3	16	C	TB	S2	26	A	TB	S1	36	D	TB	S2
7	B	TB	S2	17	A	TB	S2	27	D	TB	S2	37	A	TB	S1
8	D	TB	S4	18	D	TB	S1	28	A	TB	S1	38	C	TB	S1
9	C	TB	S3	19	B	TB	S1	29	B	TB	S1	39	A	TB	S1
10	A	TB	S2	20	D	TB	S3	30	B	TB	S1	40	A	TB	S1

Topics & Subtopics

Code	Description	Code	Description
SB1	Information & Communication Technologies	SB4	Biotechnology and Environmental Issues
SB2	Manufacturing & Construction	TB	Technology
SB3	Energy Power & Transportation		

TEST DIRECTION

DIRECTIONS

Read the questions carefully and then choose the ONE best answer to each question.

Be sure to allocate your time carefully so you are able to complete the entire test within the testing session. You may go back and review your answers at any time.

You may use any available space in your test booklet for scratch work.

Questions in this booklet are not actual test questions but they are the samples for commonly asked questions.

This test aims to cover all topics which may appear on the actual test. However some topics may not be covered.

Studying this booklet will be preparing you for the actual test. It will not guarantee improving your test score but it will help you pass your exam on the first attempt.

Some useful tips for answering multiple choice questions;

- Start with the questions that you can easily answer.

- Underline the keywords in the question.

- Be sure to read all the choices given.

- Watch for keywords such as NOT, always, only, all, never, completely.

- Do not forget to answer every question.

1

Which of the following about nanotechnology is not correct?

A) Einstein is known as the father of nanotechnology.
B) Materials produced by nanotechnology is named as nanomaterials.
C) The design of products on a molecular level is known as Nanotechnology.
D) Nanotechnology is science, engineering, and technology conducted at the nanoscale, which is about 1 to 100 nanometers.

2

A United States Department of Transportation (USDOT) hazmat placard is given above. Which of the following does it symbolize?

A) Corrosive substance
B) Electrical hazard
C) Recycling
D) Biohazard

3

David Perkins, a supporter of Gardner's theory of multiple intelligences, examined a large number of research studies both on the measurement of IQ and of programs of study designed to increase IQ.

According to Perkins, intelligence has three dimensions? Which of the following gives these components?

A) Reflective, Neural and Experiential
B) Neural, Experiential and Emotional
C) Neural, Emotional and Experiential
D) Emotional, Experiential and Reflective

4

What is the primary goal of food biotechnology?

A) To improve the health and safety of foods
B) To increase the productions of milk, meat, and other agricultural products
C) To clone agricultural products such as tomatoes
D) To develop foods for space explorations

5

Who introduced the World Wide Web (www) way back in 1991?

A) Steve Jobs
B) Dwight D. Eisenhower
C) Bill Gates
D) Tim Berners-Lee

6

Decomposing organic matter recycles various organic materials otherwise regarded as waste products.

Which of the following processes decomposes plant remains into humus by naturally occurring soil bacteria?

A) Mulching
B) Reducing
C) Conserving
D) Composting

7

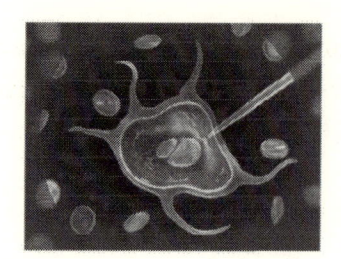

Genetic engineering, also called genetic modification, is the direct manipulation of an organism's genome using biotechnology. It is a set of technologies used to change the genetic makeup of cells, including the transfer of genes within and across species boundaries to produce improved or novel organisms.

Which of the following is a genetic engineering advancement in the medical field?

A) Gene therapy
B) Pesticides
C) Viruses
D) Good bacteria

8

Which of the following approaches has been known to give the most effective results when it comes to increasing group productivity?

A) Select a bigger team, since the pool of ideas would, therefore, be more significant.

B) Swap roles between members, therefore a supervisor wouldn't be the one always to make the last decision.

C) Select a diverse team regarding gender, ethnicity, age, and work experience.

D) Select members that together form an equilibrium of the criteria of the HBDI (Herrmann Brain Dominance Instrument) system.

9

Which of the following does "Technology in the classroom" generally mean?

A) Electric sharpeners and erasable ink

B) Gadgets and devices that students bring to school

C) Any type of technology that replaces the instructional role of teachers

D) Any type of technology, such as calculators, educational applets, etc., that serve as supplementary materials for learning

10

Which of the following is the purpose of instructional objectives?

A) To have the same ideas as the district's goals when it comes to student learning.

B) To have the school board develop you.

C) Applying teaching to students with various levels of ability.

D) To reflect each teacher's personal way of teaching.

11

In a closed electric circuit, which of the following copper wires has the smallest resistance?

A) Long wire with a large diameter
B) Long wire with a small diameter
C) Short wire with a large diameter
D) Short wire with a small diameter

12

Asperger Syndrome (AS) is a neurobiological disorder on the higher-functioning end of the autism spectrum.

Which of the following is characteristic of a child with Asperger's Syndrome?

A) The difficulty with social interactions such as speaking and forming complete sentences
B) High academic performance and cognitive development
C) Inability to acquire new information in classes such as mathematics
D) Delayed mental development and motor skills development

13

School district supplies teachers with curriculum and necessary documents.

Why should teachers still prepare annual and unit plans?

A) It is not necessary to develop annual and unit plans.
B) All school districts force teachers to write and submit annual and unit plans.
C) While preparing annual and unit plans by their own, teachers better understand what to teach.
D) Textbooks may not address all required standards, and teachers might have to supplement the curriculum.

14

Networking software is a foundational element for any network. It helps administrators deploy, manage and monitor a network.

Which country created the most used networking software in 1980's?

A) Microsoft
B) Sun
C) Novell
D) IBM

15

Bill wants to design a technology education program to help students in the development of creative solutions to current and future societal problems.

Which of the following objectives is most appropriate for Bill's program?

A) The design and construction of a 3D model for a low-income multi-dwelling unit (MDU)
B) The identification of critical equipment used in the construction of highways
C) The description of careers in construction related to home building
D) The categorization of components in a technical system

16

The internet is the global system of interconnected computer networks that use the Internet protocol suite (TCP/IP) to link devices worldwide.

Which of the following was the original purpose of the internet?

A) Global marketing and business transactions
B) The distribution of academic research papers
C) Sustaining the connectivity of US defense computers
D) Allowing people from all over the globe to easily share their thoughts and ideas

17

Which of the following is not considered as a use of standardized assessments?

A) To evaluate whether students have learned what they are expected to learn.
B) To determine whether educational policies are working as intended.
C) To identify gaps in student learning and academic progress.
D) To use standardized test results to alter classroom curriculum.

18

Which of the following terms is not defined correctly?

A) Development is the continuous process of change that all humans experience during their life.
B) Learning is the change of behaviors, thoughts or emotions based on genetics.
C) Growth is the physical process of development.
D) Maturation is the physical, emotional or intellectual process of development.

19

Which of the following does a raw score represent?

A) A family of scores that allow us to make comparisons between test scores
B) The average performance at age and grade levels
C) How close to the average, or mean the student's score fall
D) The number of items a student answers correctly without adjustment for guessing

20

The schema is an abstract concept in cognitive development, which was first used by Piaget. He emphasized the importance of schemas and described how they were developed or acquired.

Which of the following defines schema best?

A) It is a cognitive framework or concept that helps organize and interpret information.
B) It defines the process of saving knowledge in the brain.
C) It refers to the first phase of cognitive development.
D) It is a term used to explain how the brain develops.

21

What should teachers keep in mind when designing instruction?

A) Not all kids are on the same level.
B) All students understand the same way.
C) Instructional planning isn't as crucial as it is believed.
D) The previous experiences of students aren't the base of learning.

22

Which of the following about the assessment is not true?

A) The most significant quality of a good assessment is validity.
B) An assessment is a process of gathering information from multiple sources to understand what students know, understand, and can do with their knowledge.
C) A standardized test is any form of test that requires all test takers to answer the same questions from a common bank of questions.
D) While interpreting raw scores, knowledge of basic statistics is essential.

23

For research data to be of value and use, they must be both reliable and valid. Reliability refers to the repeatability of findings and validity refers to the credibility or believability of the research.

Which of the following defines validity?

A) The degree to which an assessment tool produces stable and consistent results
B) The extent to which a test accurately measures what it is supposed to measure
C) The extent to which an assessment measures the achievement of desired objectives
D) The extent to which an assessment covers all the items that have been taught or studied

24

Gestalt psychology is a movement in psychology founded in Germany in 1912. It is an attempt to understand the laws behind the ability to acquire and maintain meaningful perceptions in a chaotic world.

Which of the following statements would be in agreement with Gestalt theory?

A) Single notes must remain constant to recognize an overall melody
B) Pieces of a puzzle take priority over the total image
C) Perceptual experience is more than the sum of its elements
D) Slower the image projection faster the perception of movement

25

By using which type of performance assessment can a teacher understand what the students are able to do for long periods of time?

A) Extended performance assessment
B) Individual performance assessment
C) Restricted-response performance assessment
D) Authentic performance assessment

26

The curriculum can be defined as the totality of student experiences that occur in the educational process.

Which of the following about curriculum is not correct?

A) Curriculum planning is essential because it makes classroom discipline easier.
B) A curriculum map is an ever-evolving document that should generally be followed based on the needs of the students.
C) Big ideas are important in curriculum planning because it helps the teacher figure out what's most important about a curriculum.
D) Modern curriculum models are often a blend of process and product.

27

Which of the following situations demonstrates the productive use of technology as classroom tools?

A) Showing funny movies to students during their free time
B) Encouraging the use of social media among teachers and students
C) Using technology to keep students busy
D) Using interactive whiteboards in teaching interactive lessons; showing presentations to aid teaching

28

A computer virus is a piece of code that is capable of copying itself and typically has a detrimental effect, such as corrupting the system or destroying data.

In 1983, who was the first to offer a definition of the term 'computer virus'?

A) Norton
B) Cohen
C) Mcafee
D) Smith

29

An email address identifies the email box to which email messages are delivered. An email address is made up of a local-part, an @ symbol, then a case-insensitive domain.

In which year was the @ chosen for its use in an email address?

A) 1972
B) 1976
C) 1980
D) 1984

30

Several instructors are developing software with the goal of improving students' drafting skills.

Which of the following is the first appropriate step that the instructors should take?

A) Determine the learning objectives intended for the software
B) Download the most widely used software for evaluation
C) Decide the most appropriate user interface (UI) for the software
D) Determine the importance of drafting skills through a survey

31

Which of the following about Observations and Inferences is not correct?

A) Observations are mere generalizations; inferences are eye-witness accounts.
B) Observations are based on information seen; inferences are based on information already known.
C) Observations may skew the truth; inferences reveal the true state regardless of speaker's claims.
D) All of these answers are correct.

CONTINUE ▶

32

Which of the following about development is not correct?

A) B.F. Skinner has contributed to the behaviorist perspective of Educational Psychology.
B) Learning how to do addition is an example of cognitive development.
C) Environment influences a person's genes. This belief is an example of the interaction of DNA and heredity.
D) Emotional development is about understanding emotions while social development is about learning to interact with others.

33

Which of the following is not a correct explanation?

A) Metacognition means thinking and learning about one's thinking and learning processes.
B) The schema is a term used by Piaget referring to a mental construct that one forms to understand the environment.
C) Assimilation happens when the existing schema needs to be modified to take in new information.
D) Self-efficacy is a term used by Bandura for self-confidence in one's ability to complete a specific task.

34

Communication Cycle refers to the transfer of information from one person to the another through a proper cycle.

Which of the following is an essential component of communication cycle?

A) A message
B) An email account
C) An internet connection
D) An interpreter

35

A student would want to use technology as a learning tool throughout the school year.

Which is the best example of how this student can accomplish this goal?

A) Make a poster to illustrate the student's ideas about an article.
B) The student uses a smartphone to call a tutor to help her answer a quiz.
C) The student makes a report and a presentation on her computer.
D) The student uses the references found in her textbook to find additional resources for a project.

36

An effective teacher engages all students and provides a learning environment where all students can learn.

Which of the following is a strategy used in effective teaching?

A) Getting feedback from students and motivating them
B) Promoting student interest and giving plenty of examples to clarify the topic
C) Breaking complex material down and making complicated topics easy to understand
D) All of the above

37

By considering which of the following first can a teacher prepare an effective lesson for a new instructional unit?

A) Unit activities best for individual and group work
B) The most efficient way to evaluate students' achievement of unit objectives
C) Background knowledge the students already have with regard to the unit topic
D) The ways unit supports the goals of the district curriculum in this subject area

38

Communication is exchanging information by speaking, writing, or using some other medium.

Which of the following is not correct about communication?

A) Nonverbal communication is the use of body movements to send a message.
B) If a speaker uses graphs, charts he is using an assertion of logic.
C) It is never appropriate to use obscene language in a speech.
D) Pitch has a psychological effect that influences how people perceive your speech's content.

39

The teacher always begins regular class meetings by giving individual students an opportunity to thank a classmate for assistance with a difficult or challenging task.

Which of the following outcomes does it have to begin a class meeting in this way?

A) High expectations for their learning
B) Students' self-monitoring of their own behavior
C) A supportive and caring classroom community
D) A positive learning environment that fosters excellence

Computer software is a set of instructions and associated documentation that tells a computer what to do or how to perform a task.

An English language learner is searching for computer software to help him make connections between written and spoken English. Which of the following types of computer software would be most useful?

A) Automated translation
B) Word prediction
C) Speech synthesizer
D) Sound recording

SECTION 2 - EDUCATION

#	Answer	Topic	Subtopic	#	Answer	Topic	Subtopic	#	Answer	Topic	Subtopic	#	Answer	Topic	Subtopic
1	A	TA	SA1	11	C	TB	SB3	21	A	TA	SA2	31	C	TA	SA2
2	A	TA	SA1	12	A	TA	SA2	22	D	TA	SA2	32	C	TA	SA2
3	A	TA	SA2	13	D	TA	SA2	23	B	TA	SA2	33	C	TA	SA2
4	A	TB	SB4	14	C	TA	SA1	24	C	TA	SA2	34	A	TA	SA1
5	D	TA	SA1	15	A	TA	SA2	25	A	TA	SA2	35	C	TA	SA2
6	D	TB	SB4	16	C	TA	SA1	26	A	TA	SA2	36	D	TA	SA2
7	A	TB	SB4	17	D	TA	SA2	27	D	TA	SA2	37	C	TA	SA2
8	D	TA	SA2	18	B	TA	SA2	28	B	TA	SA1	38	D	TA	SA1
9	D	TA	SA2	19	D	TA	SA2	29	A	TA	SA1	39	C	TA	SA2
10	A	TA	SA2	20	A	TA	SA2	30	A	TA	SA2	40	C	TA	SA2

Topics & Subtopics

Code	Description
SA1	Technology & Society
SA2	Pedagogical & Professional Studies
SB3	Energy Power & Transportation

Code	Description
SB4	Biotechnology and Environmental Issues
TA	Education
TB	Technology

TEST DIRECTION

DIRECTIONS

Read the questions carefully and then choose the ONE best answer to each question.

Be sure to allocate your time carefully so you are able to complete the entire test within the testing session. You may go back and review your answers at any time.

You may use any available space in your test booklet for scratch work.

Questions in this booklet are not actual test questions but they are the samples for commonly asked questions.

This test aims to cover all topics which may appear on the actual test. However some topics may not be covered.

Studying this booklet will be preparing you for the actual test. It will not guarantee improving your test score but it will help you pass your exam on the first attempt.

Some useful tips for answering multiple choice questions;

- Start with the questions that you can easily answer.

- Underline the keywords in the question.

- Be sure to read all the choices given.

- Watch for keywords such as NOT, always, only, all, never, completely.

- Do not forget to answer every question.

1

Which type of engineer among the following is most likely involved in the planning of a massive dam's construction?

A) Systems engineer
B) Architectural engineer
C) Mechanical engineer
D) Civil engineer

2

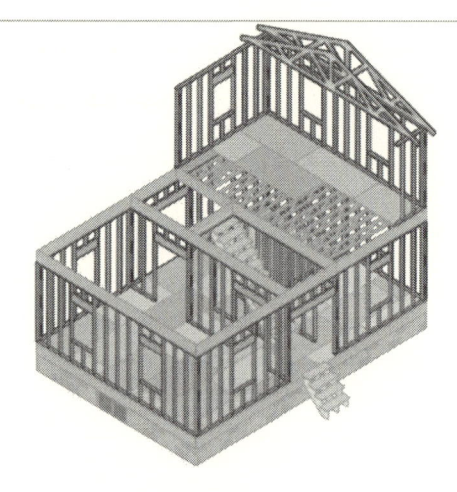

Which of the following is the structure that provides vertical support for the construction of a house?

A) Headers
B) Studs
C) Joists
D) Rafters

3

A protocol is a standard used to define a method of exchanging data over a computer network.

Which of the protocols given below is used for sending email?

A) HTTP
B) TCP/IP
C) SMTP
D) FTP

4

Which of the following would be the first step in the design process a doghouse?

A) Purchasing the required materials for building
B) Determine the measurement of the dog and the materials for the interior
C) Acquiring the necessary tools for building
D) Identifying the aesthetic concerns of the exterior

5

Which type of engineer among the following is most likely involved in the designing of an electric generator?

A) Systems engineer
B) Architectural engineer
C) Mechanical engineer
D) Civil engineer

6

How can you successfully convert an image from BMP to JPEG format?

A) By changing the image file extension
B) By compressing the file
C) By using the "Save As" command
D) By renaming the image

7

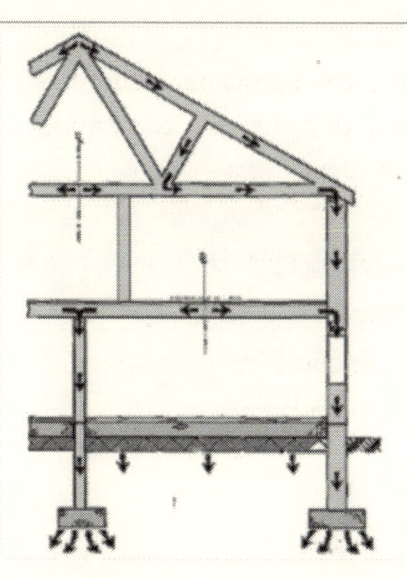

Which type of wall provides the support needed to withstand weight from a building's ceiling and roof?

A) Stud-support
B) Rafter-plate
C) Load-bearing
D) Ceiling-joist

8

An output device is any device used to send data from a computer to another device or user.

Which of the following is not an output device?

A) Plotter
B) Printer
C) Monitor
D) Touchscreen

9

Which of the following is the encoding of the signal that travels from a television remote to the television?

A) Visible light pulse
B) Series of intense infrared beams
C) Series of infrared pulses
D) Radio wave signal

10

The key concepts of guidance, control, suspension, propulsion, and support are taught in which of the following areas?

A) Biotechnical systems
B) Integrated systems
C) Transportation
D) Manufacturing

11

Which of the following is acceptable according to design specifications indicating a width of 8.00 cm ± 0.05 cm and a length of 14.95 cm ± 0.10 cm?

A) 7.90 cm × 15.00 cm
B) 7.95 cm × 15.05 cm
C) 7.95 cm × 15.10 cm
D) 7.90 cm × 15.10 cm

12

Both pneumatics and hydraulics are applications of fluid power.

Which of the following about pneumatics and hydraulics is not correct?

A) Pneumatics uses an easily compressible gas such as air.
B) Hydraulics uses relatively incompressible liquid media such as oil.
C) Pneumatic systems generally have long operating lives and require little maintenance.
D) Hydraulics supply less power than pneumatics.

13

For which of the following purposes do metal workers use press brake?

A) Bending
B) Forging
C) Grinding
D) Welding

14

Which of the following violates the copyright law when someone buys an image-editing software?

A) Copying the software onto a disk for a friend
B) Selling the software and the software's disk to a third party
C) Copying the software's disk to make a backup
D) Creating artwork with the application and selling it

15

Why is using a network switch more preferable than using a network hub?

A) Because a network switch reduces the network traffic
B) Because a network switch connects a computer directly to the internet
C) Because a network switch prevents all viruses from spreading
D) Because a network switch strengthens password security

16

A flexible manufacturing system (FMS) is a manufacturing system in which there is some amount of flexibility that allows the system to react in case of changes, whether predicted or unpredicted.

The roots of a flexible manufacturing system were laid by Jerome H. Lemelson (1923-97), an American inventor with a master's degree in Industrial Engineering.

Which of the following about FMS is not correct?

A) It has low up-front cost but the costs of operation are high.
B) Specialized labor is needed to run, monitor and maintain the FMS
C) It gives manufacturing firms an advantage to quickly change a manufacturing environment
D) Machines and computerized systems are configured to manufacture different parts and handle varying levels of production.

CONTINUE ▶

17

A computer storage device is any type of hardware that stores data.

Which of the following storage devices allows access to information in a sequential mode?

A) Hard disk
B) DVD
C) CD-R
D) Magnetic tape

18

Which of the following is not correct?

A) Gasoline engines use a spark plug, and diesel engines do not.
B) Gasoline engines have a higher compression ratio than diesel engines.
C) If a gas engine turns over well, but it fails to start you should check for spark at the plug.
D) A circuit breaker protects an electrical circuit against excessive ampere flow.

19

Which of the following results in data for preproduction processes in advanced manufacturing?

A) Run-sequence plot
B) Range chart
C) Pareto chart
D) X-bar chart

20

In a manufacturing laboratory, a student asks his teacher what assembly procedures should be used when solving a fabrication problem.

Which of the following would be the teacher's best response?

A) Provide possible assembly procedures for the student to select
B) Ask the student to make their own judgment and decide
C) Provide an opinion on the best assembly procedure for the problem
D) Use leading questions to guide the student in analyzing the merits of different assembly procedures

CONTINUE ▶

21

The traditional manufacturing process is known for its products being made in batches. Production of the product moves from one stage to the next stage one piece at a time. One piece movement benefits the manufacturer because there is no idle time between the units.

What is this process also known as?

A) One-piece flow
B) Flexible manufacturing
C) Automatic manufacturing
D) Multiple flows

22

The Open Systems Interconnection model is a conceptual model that defines the communication functions of a telecommunication or computing system without regard to their underlying internal structure and technology.

In which of the following layers of the Open Systems Interconnection model is wireless network technology implemented?

A) Session
B) Data link
C) Application
D) Physical

23

A MAC address is a hardware identification number that identifies each device on a network. The MAC address is manufactured into every network card and cannot be changed.

Which of the following defines MAC?

A) Memory Address Corruption
B) Media Access Code
C) Mediocre Apple Computer
D) Media Access Control

24

It is used for connecting a local area network using one protocol with a wide area network applying a different protocol. It performs the traffic directing functions on the Internet.

Which of the following is explained above?

A) Switch
B) Hub
C) Router
D) Server

25

In computer hardware and software development, testing is used at critical checkpoints in the overall process to determine whether objectives are being met.

Which of the following is NOT a type of testing?

A) Sample Checking
B) Manual Testing with sample data
C) Testing by a group of users
D) Testing sample data on the computer

26

An error is a term used to describe any issue that arises unexpectedly that cause a computer to not function properly.

What kind of an error is the omission of a semicolon at the end of a statement in C++?

A) Syntax
B) Calculation
C) Loop
D) Direct

27

In contrast to finite energy sources like fossil fuels, renewable energy sources naturally regenerate over time.

Which of the following is an example of a renewable energy source?

A) Oil
B) Coal
C) Natural gas
D) Wood

28

A third-generation programming language is a generational way to categorize high-level computer programming languages.

Which of the following is NOT a 3rd generation programming language?

A) FORTRAN
B) Java
C) ADA
D) Assembly Language

29

SSL is the standard security technology for establishing an encrypted link between a web server and a browser. This link ensures that all data passed between the web server and browsers remain private and integral.

What does SSL stand for?

A) Secure system login
B) System socket layer
C) Secure socket layer
D) Secure system login

30

Boolean data type is a data type with only two possible values: true or false.

A variable of type Boolean would be most appropriate to store the result of which of the following?

A) Arithmetic calculation
B) Concatenation
C) Formatting
D) Object creation

31

Signature-based detection methods refer to the methods for the detection of attacks by looking for specific patterns, such as byte sequences in network traffic, or known malicious instruction sequences used by malware.

Which of the following is the greatest drawback of this detection method?

A) Block incoming data from the network server
B) Fail to identify new or unknown viruses
C) Require frequent scans of all executable files
D) Delete essential files that are not infected

32

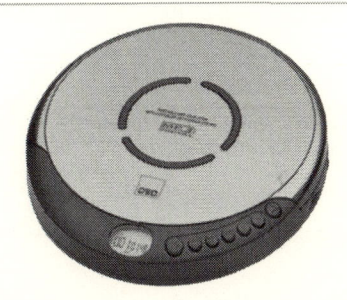

A CD player is an electronic device to play an audio compact disc which is a digital optical disc data storage format.

Which of the following does the CD audio player use for reproducing sound?

A) Titanium Needle
B) Barium Titanium Ceramic
C) Laser Beam
D) Quartz Crystal

CONTINUE ▶

33

There are six major categories of computers which are based on differences in size, speed, processing capabilities, and price.

In which category of computers do desktop computers, notebooks (laptops) and Personal Digital Assistants (PDA's) fall?

A) Microcomputers
B) Supercomputers
C) Mainframe computers
D) Minicomputers

34

Computer data is the information processed or stored by a computer such as documents, text, images, audio clips, software programs, or other types of data.

How is computer data represented inside the computer?

A) Byte system
B) Binary system
C) Hexadecimal system
D) Logical System

35

A translator is a computer program that performs the translation of a program written in a given programming language into a functionally equivalent program in different ways without losing the functional structure of the original code.

Which of the following is the translator that converts high-level languages before the programme is executed?

A) Compiler
B) Query language
C) BASIC
D) Interpreter

An algorithm is a process or set of rules to be followed in calculations or other problem-solving operations, primarily by a computer.

A student has a horizontal list of numbered cards, and he sorts them manually by moving the cards in the sequence below.

1. Find the smallest card in the list and exchange it with the first card in the list.

2. Find the next smallest card in the list and exchange it with the second card in the list.

3. Repeat these instructions until the original list is sorted.

Which of the following algorithms is described above?

A) Merge sort
B) Selection sort
C) Bubble sort
D) Insertion sort

SECTION 3 - TECHNOLOGY

#	Answer	Topic	Subtopic	#	Answer	Topic	Subtopic	#	Answer	Topic	Subtopic	#	Answer	Topic	Subtopic
1	D	TB	S2	10	C	TB	S2	19	A	TB	S2	28	D	TB	S1
2	B	TB	S2	11	B	TB	S2	20	D	TB	S2	29	C	TB	S1
3	C	TB	S1	12	D	TB	S2	21	A	TB	S2	30	D	TB	S1
4	B	TB	S2	13	A	TB	S2	22	D	TB	S1	31	B	TB	S1
5	C	TB	S2	14	A	TB	S1	23	D	TB	S1	32	C	TB	S1
6	C	TB	S1	15	A	TB	S1	24	C	TB	S1	33	A	TB	S1
7	C	TB	S2	16	A	TB	S2	25	B	TB	S1	34	B	TB	S1
8	D	TB	S1	17	D	TB	S1	26	A	TB	S1	35	A	TB	S1
9	C	TB	S1	18	B	TB	S3	27	D	TB	S3	36	B	TB	S1

Topics & Subtopics

Code	Description	Code	Description
SB1	Information & Communication Technologies	SB3	Energy Power & Transportation
SB2	Manufacturing & Construction	TB	Technology

TEST DIRECTION

DIRECTIONS

Read the questions carefully and then choose the ONE best answer to each question.

Be sure to allocate your time carefully so you are able to complete the entire test within the testing session. You may go back and review your answers at any time.

You may use any available space in your test booklet for scratch work.

Questions in this booklet are not actual test questions but they are the samples for commonly asked questions.

This test aims to cover all topics which may appear on the actual test. However some topics may not be covered.

Studying this booklet will be preparing you for the actual test. It will not guarantee improving your test score but it will help you pass your exam on the first attempt.

Some useful tips for answering multiple choice questions;

- Start with the questions that you can easily answer.

- Underline the keywords in the question.

- Be sure to read all the choices given.

- Watch for keywords such as NOT, always, only, all, never, completely.

- Do not forget to answer every question.

1

Which of the following is not a correct definition?

A) Internet addressing is developed in 1984 and named as Domain Name System (DNS)

B) A web address is also known as Uniform Resource Locator (URL)

C) The protocol for transferring web files is known as Hypertext Transfer Protocol (HTTP)

D) Hypertext Markup Language (HTML) is an operating system that transfers data to and from a hard drive

2

A teacher has implemented learning objectives for a unit of study. Which of the following steps should the teacher take next?

A) Put in order the activities to help students meet the learning objectives.

B) Determine how to evaluate students' mastery of the learning objectives.

C) Identify skills that students will need to develop in meeting the learning objectives.

D) Implement strategies for presenting concepts related to the learning objectives.

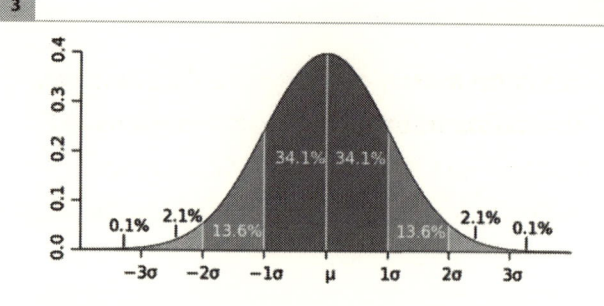

3

Which of the following does a measurement showing the "average differences" from what most people score on a test refer to?

A) Mean
B) Mode
C) Median
D) Standard deviation

4

CRM is a technology for managing all your company's interactions with customers and potential customers.

What does the acronym CRM mean?

A) Customer Relationship Management
B) Customer's Relative Meet
C) Customer Retention Manager
D) Channel Root Market Customer

5

A vision statement is a school's roadmap, indicating both what the school wants to become and guiding transformational initiatives by setting a defined direction for the school's growth.

What does an effective vision statement focus on?

A) Promotion of community diversity
B) Teamwork between teachers and students
C) Continuous professional development of the school's teachers and other staff
D) High expectations for student learning

6

Which of the following assessment methods would be the best for the year-long evaluation of student's drafting skills development?

A) Teacher-created assessment
B) Short-answer unit assessment
C) Baseline assessment
D) Portfolio assessment

7

Which factor has been most responsible for decisions to place greater emphasis on developing students' problem-solving and decision-making skills across the curriculum?

A) The increasing influence of media in teaching and learning
B) The change in occupational demands in both local and global societies
C) The increase in educational accountability of every school
D) The change in inclusion practices in every school

8

What is the reason behind the importance of the Green Revolution in modern times ever since it was developed in the early 1900s?

A) It raised global support for environmental preservation initiatives.
B) It encouraged the development and use of renewable energy sources.
C) It aggressively advocated for equal rights for women and children.
D) It increased crop yields to combat starvation in developing nations.

Multiple types of processes used by a manufacturer can be grouped in the four main categories; casting and molding, machining, joining, and shearing and forming.

Which of the following about these manufacturing types is not correct?

A) Casting is a popular type of molding which involves heating plastic until it becomes liquid, then pouring it into a mold.
B) In the machining process, tools like saws, sheers and rotating wheels are used by manufacturers to make products.
C) To put multiple parts together to make one piece, manufacturers use joining processes like welding and soldering to apply heat to combine materials. Parts can also be joined by using adhesives or fasteners.
D) Forming uses cutting blades to make straight cuts into a piece of metal and shearing uses compression or another type of stress to give materials the desired shape.

Which of the following assessments measure a student's ability to learn in a certain situation?

A) CBM (Curriculum-Based Measure)
B) Diagnostic assessment
C) Dynamic assessment
D) An aptitude test

11

A rural school seeks to increase its access to technological resources for teaching and learning. However, the school is significantly experiencing funding problems.

Which action should the school administrators do to achieve this goal?

A) Collaborate with educators from the more affluent and technologically advanced schools to learn various strategies.
B) Seek support from local businesses that may have interest in having partnerships in achieving the school's goal.
C) Cut other areas of the school's budget plan and use it to increase the technology funding.
D) Solicit for public assistance in raising funds for the school through publicizing its needs in newspapers and other local media.

12

By adopting the Common Core Standards, which of the following state commitment does a school most directly reflect?

A) Ensuring accountability for teachers, schools, and districts
B) Guaranteeing that graduates have the knowledge and skills needed for college or career success
C) Delivering culturally responsive instructions and address the students' diverse needs
D) Strengthening collaboration with other states to improve learning achievement

13

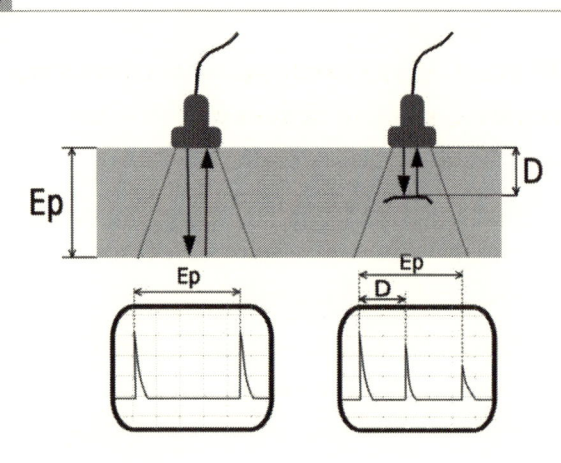

There are different procedures for analyzing material properties. **Ultrasonic Testing (UT)** is a form of nondestructive testing which utilizes propagation of high-frequency ultrasonic sound waves to detect cracks and defects in parts and materials as they move through a material.

Which of the following about Ultrasonic Testing (UT) is not correct?

A) It is highly accurate in estimating the size and shape of the material.
B) It can be used to determine a material's thickness, such as measuring the wall thickness of a pipe.
C) Materials that are irregular in shape, very thin or not homogeneous are difficult to inspect with UT.
D) In industrial applications, ultrasonic testing is widely used on engineering materials such as metals, plastics, composites, ceramics, wood and paper products.

14

A teacher states "Technology is great! Using technology in every lesson keeps the kids so occupied!"

Because of which of the following you should not agree with that teacher's comment?

A) Technology should be used as an enhancement and supplement to effective teaching and learning
B) Technology should never be used for instruction but only as a recreational tool
C) Technology should not be used as often as possible
D) Technology distracts students and hinders learning

15

Curriculum guides are documents used by states, school districts and individual schools to guide teachers in their instruction. Many guides are detailed, giving teachers a specific scope of what to teach and when. Many provide additional resources, such as necessary materials and assessment tools.

Which of the following about curriculum guides is not correct?

A) It helps teachers decide what to teach and when
B) It can be based on grade level of students.
C) It can not be based on the number of students in each class.
D) It helps teachers decide on classroom management strategies.

16

When selecting reading materials to support the concepts presented in a lesson, a teacher should ask which of the following questions first?

A) Are these materials usable for more than one lesson presentation?
B) Will students require additional instruction to use these materials effectively?
C) Do these materials support a variety of student groupings?
D) Are these materials consistent with the students' comprehension and skill levels?

17

Which of the following about intelligence and creativity development of a child is not correct?

A) Gardner proposed The Theory of Multiple Intelligences.
B) Intelligence remains stable, but IQ scores drop with age.
C) The Fagan test evaluates an infant's intelligence through her socio-motor skills.
D) IQ scores fluctuate during adolescence.

18

The Cold War is the name given to the relationship that developed primarily between the USA and the USSR after World War Two. The Cold War was to dominate international affairs for decades, and many significant crises occurred, such as the Cuban Missile Crisis, Vietnam, Hungary and the Berlin Wall is just some.

Which technology advanced the most during this period?

A) Information
B) Agricultural
C) Manufacturing
D) Military and science

CONTINUE ▶

19

Antibiotics are medicines used to treat a wide variety of infections or diseases caused by bacteria, such as respiratory tract infections, urinary tract infections, skin infections and infected wounds. Antibiotics have had both positive and negative impacts on society.

Which of the following can be considered as a negative impact of antibiotics?

A) New types of cancers have developed due to extensive use of antibiotics.
B) Over-abundance of medical professionals.
C) Increased obesity in humans due to use in consumer products.
D) Resistant strains of bacteria caused by extensive use of antibiotics.

20

Student-centered learning is also known as learner-centered education. In student-centered learning, methods of teaching shift the focus of instruction from the teacher to the student so that students move from passive receivers of information to active participants in their own discovery process.

Which of the following defines the role of a teacher in a student-centered environment?

A) Law enforcer who makes sure students are following the rules and regulations.
B) Co-teacher who works alongside the students to deliver lessons.
C) The organizer who monitors and supports student activities.
D) A dictator who tells students what to do and controls all their actions.

21

A manufacturing system is a method of organizing production. Many types of manufacturing systems are in place, including assembly lines, batch production, and computer-integrated manufacturing, or even mass production manufacturing and custom manufacturing.

Which of the following given below is an advantage of using mass production over custom manufacturing?

A) Workers can learn important skills.
B) Faster production and lower cost.
C) Feedback can be provided to the workers by customers.
D) Certain products can be more easily modified at the request of customers.

22

Creativity development is a nonlinear and multifaceted process starting early in life.

Which of the following about creativity development and intelligence of a child is not correct?

A) Sternberg proposed The Triarchic Theory
B) The Torrance Test can assess Child's creativity
C) Adoption studies show evidence of a genetic influence on intelligence
D) Crystallized intelligence refers to the knowledge that remains stable over the years

23

Regarding the social development of nine-year-old students, which of the following teaching strategies is likely to have the most positive influence?

A) Emphasizing student-led activities
B) Encouraging students during challenging activities
C) Giving a chance for students to express their feelings freely in the classroom
D) Assigning cooperative rather than competitive student activities

24

A computer company is a commercial entity involved in the computer industry. Which American computer company is called Big Blue?

A) IBM
B) Tandy Svenson
C) Compaq Corp
D) Microsoft

25

A soldering iron supplies heat to melt solder so that it can flow into the joint between two workpieces. What is the best way on cleaning the tip of a soldering iron?

A) Scraping the tip against a wet sponge after the iron is thoroughly heated
B) Using a metal file to file off the remaining solder
C) Submerging the tip in hot soapy water overnight
D) Soaking the iron in flux for a few hours before each use

26

Which of the following about basic terms of development is not correct?

A) Nurture refers to the effect of the environment upon a person.
B) Nature refers to the traits that are inherited.
C) Maturation is limitless but Growth is limited.
D) Learning new skills is an example of growth.

27

Demographic transition (DT) refers to the transition from high birth and death rates to lower birth and death rates as a country or region develops from a pre-industrial to an industrialized economic system.

Which of the following given below can be considered as a supposition of the demographic transition theory?

A) Innovation and increased productivity are being promoted by population growths.
B) Levels of population and resources are proportional to rates of population growth.
C) A society's levels of technological and economic development are reflected by population patterns.
D) Food supplies increase arithmetically, and human population increases geometrically.

28

Electronic mail (email) is a method of exchanging messages between people using electronics.

Which of the following statements is correct about the first email in history?

A) David Crocker sent the first email in 1963
B) Gregor Maxwell sent the first email in 1969
C) Ray Tomlinson sent the first email in 1971
D) Gray Tomlinson sent the first email in 1974

29

Which of the following organizations could help a high school teacher to pursue professional development opportunities for integrating computational thinking and programming concepts into his class?

A) Computer Science Teachers Association
B) Special Interest Group on Computer Science Education
C) Association for the Advancement of Computing in Education
D) International Society for Technology in Education

30

A hard drive is a non-volatile memory hardware device that permanently stores and retrieves data on a computer. The IBM PC-XT was the first to include a hard drive.

What was the capacity of this disk?

A) 1.44 KB
B) 10 KB
C) 750 KB
D) 20 KB

31

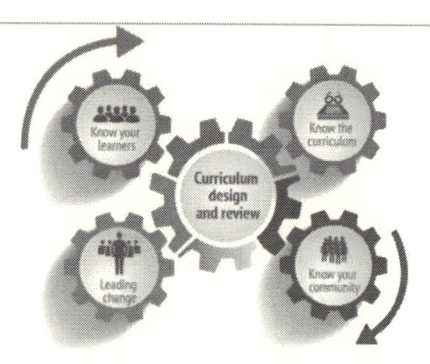

Curriculum design is a statement which identifies the elements of the curriculum, and shows what their relationships are to each other. It also indicates the principles and the requirements of organization for the regulatory conditions under which it is to operate.

Which of the following about curriculum design is not correct?

A) The curriculum is the stuff teachers teach.
B) Curriculum models provide a framework for curriculum guides.
C) Backward design in curriculum planning is designing the end of the day before creating the beginning of the day.
D) Curriculum planning helps to make sure teaching on a daily basis has a larger purpose.

32

Vygotsky is an educational psychologist who is well known for his sociocultural theory. According to this theory, social interaction leads to continuous step-by-step changes in children's thought and behavior that can vary significantly from culture to culture.

Which of the following about cognitive development and Vygotsky's theory is not correct?

A) Vygotsky used a sociocultural perspective in his theory of cognitive development.
B) Staying cognitively active is helpful for maintaining both fluid and crystallized intelligence.
C) According to Vygotsky, scaffolding is the process of constructing an internal representation of external physical objects or actions.
D) Lev Vygotsky is most well-known for a cultural-historical theory of cognitive development emphasizing social interactions and culture.

33

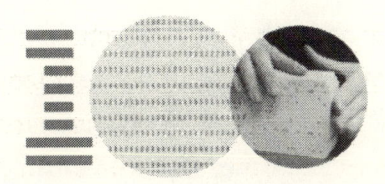

A punch card is a piece of stiff paper that can be used to contain digital information represented by the presence or absence of holes in predefined positions.

Who is credited with the idea of using punch cards to control patterns in a weaving machine?

A) Hollerith
B) Babbage
C) Pascal
D) Jacquard

34

Ms. Doldi is being interviewed for a teaching position. The school principal asked her how technology can be a useful tool for students.

Which of the following ideas should Ms. Doldi respond to give the most accurate and complete answer?

A) Technology can be used to replace the instructional role of teachers, for practicing academic skills, and for playing games.
B) Technology can be used to make learning fun, to access social media, and for practicing academic skills.
C) Technology can be used as a tool for learning new things, demonstrating knowledge and practicing academic skills.
D) Technology can be used as a tool for learning new things.

35

Educational Psychology is the study of how humans learn and retain knowledge, primarily in educational settings like classrooms. It includes social, emotional and cognitive learning processes.

Which of the following about Educational Psychology is not correct?

A) The responsibility of learning falls on the learner rather than the teacher according to the Constructivist perspective.
B) Albert Bandura contributed a lot to the Social-Cognitive Educational Psychology.
C) Learning occurs through stage-like processes according to the Developmental Educational Psychology.
D) Learning occurs through observation according to the Cognitive Educational Psychology.

36

A rubric is typically an evaluation tool or set of guidelines used to promote the consistent application of learning expectations, learning objectives, or learning standards in the classroom, or to measure their attainment against a consistent set of criteria.

A teacher would like to develop a rubric for assessing students' computer programs that students will be able to explain how their programs work. Which of the following rubric components could be most effective?

A) The code variables are declared using the correct data types.
B) The program outputs the correct solution to the problem.
C) The program compiles without any syntax or runtime errors.
D) The code contains clear and appropriate internal documentation.

SECTION 4 - EDUCATION

#	Answer	Topic	Subtopic	#	Answer	Topic	Subtopic	#	Answer	Topic	Subtopic	#	Answer	Topic	Subtopic
1	D	TB	SB1	10	C	TA	SA2	19	D	TA	SA1	28	C	TA	SA1
2	C	TA	SA2	11	B	TA	SA1	20	C	TA	SA2	29	A	TA	SA2
3	D	TA	SA2	12	B	TA	SA2	21	B	TA	SA1	30	B	TA	SA1
4	A	TA	SA1	13	D	TB	SB3	22	D	TA	SA2	31	C	TA	SA2
5	D	TA	SA1	14	A	TA	SA2	23	D	TA	SA2	32	C	TA	SA2
6	D	TA	SA2	15	D	TA	SA2	24	A	TA	SA1	33	D	TA	SA1
7	B	TA	SA1	16	D	TA	SA2	25	A	TB	SB2	34	C	TA	SA2
8	D	TA	SA1	17	C	TA	SA2	26	D	TA	SA2	35	D	TA	SA2
9	D	TB	SB2	18	D	TA	SA1	27	C	TA	SA1	36	D	TA	SA2

Topics & Subtopics

Code	Description
SA1	Technology & Society
SA2	Pedagogical & Professional Studies
SB1	Information & Communication Technologies
SB2	Manufacturing & Construction

Code	Description
SB3	Energy Power & Transportation
TA	Education
TB	Technology

TEST DIRECTION

DIRECTIONS

Read the questions carefully and then choose the ONE best answer to each question.

Be sure to allocate your time carefully so you are able to complete the entire test within the testing session. You may go back and review your answers at any time.

You may use any available space in your test booklet for scratch work.

Questions in this booklet are not actual test questions but they are the samples for commonly asked questions.

This test aims to cover all topics which may appear on the actual test. However some topics may not be covered.

Studying this booklet will be preparing you for the actual test. It will not guarantee improving your test score but it will help you pass your exam on the first attempt.

Some useful tips for answering multiple choice questions;

- Start with the questions that you can easily answer.

- Underline the keywords in the question.

- Be sure to read all the choices given.

- Watch for keywords such as NOT, always, only, all, never, completely.

- Do not forget to answer every question.

1.

Which of the following the potential difference of an external circuit that has a current of 2.0 Ampere and a resistance of 7.0 Ohm?

A) 9.0 V
B) 0.28 V
C) 14.0 V
D) 3.5 V

2.

In what way are science and technology related?

A) Science and technology are not related, each deal with separate things.
B) Technology is the application of scientific knowledge for practical purposes in the society.
C) Science is the application of technology for practical purposes in the society.
D) None of the above.

3.

Which of the following defines engineering?

A) A branch of science and technology that deals with designing, building and using structures and machines.
B) A branch of science that deals with investigating the fundamental laws of the universe.
C) A branch of science that deals with the operations of machines.
D) None of the above.

4.

Which of the following is an example of the power system used in an early 19th-century railway steam locomotive engines?

A) Reaction engine
B) Internal combustion (IC) engine
C) External combustion (EC) engine
D) Rotary engine

CONTINUE ▶

5

Which of the following about system diagrams is not correct?

A) System Diagrams include feedback loops.
B) System Diagrams are exactly the same as the flowcharts.
C) A systems diagram helps you to understand how complex systems work.
D) A system diagram is a visual model of a system, its components, and their interactions.

6

Which of the following statements is not correct?

A) Power is the ability to do work.
B) The conversion of organic materials to energy is known as Biomass Energy.
C) A British thermal unit (Btu) is defined as the amount of energy required to raise 1 pound of water 1°F.
D) Petroleum, coal, and wood are similar in that they are all forms of stored energy found in nature.

7

Statistical Process Control (SPC) is an industry-standard methodology for measuring and controlling quality during the manufacturing process.

Which of the following is not a purpose of the control chart in the statistical process control (SPC)?

A) It helps to determine the capability of the process.
B) It is an essential tool for continuous quality control.
C) It helps to identify the factors that impede peak performance.
D) It predicts the demand for a manufactured product under various economic conditions.

8

Which of the following explains why wind energy is viewed as a type of solar energy?

A) Solar energy is accountable for wind energy.
B) Areas rich in solar energy are also rich in wind energy.
C) Both solar and wind energies are acquired from atmospheric conditions.
D) Both solar and wind energies are renewable.

9

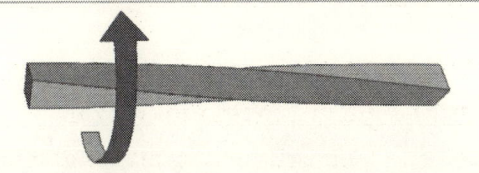

Mechanical stress is a measure of internal forces that arise in a body being deformed as a result of external forces. The image above depicts a type of mechanical stress.

Which of the following does the image denote?

A) Torsion
B) Compression
C) Shear
D) Tension

10

In a large-scale commercial construction venture, which of the following is normally the first step that needs to be taken?

A) Applying for building permits and variances
B) Holding a discussion with the developer, designer, and contractor regarding the scope of the construction
C) Ordering the necessary materials for building the foundation
D) Drafting a contract specifying details of the building plan

11

If the voltage between two points in a circuit is 5,000 volts, which of the following can be correct about this simple circuit?

A) It has a current of 20 amperes and a resistance of 250 ohms.
B) It has a current of 20 amperes and a resistance of 100,000 ohms.
C) It has a current of 20 ohms and a resistance of 250 amperes.
D) It has a current of 100,000 amperes and a resistance of 20 ohms.

12

A truss bridge is a bridge whose load-bearing superstructure is composed of a truss, a structure of connected elements.

Which of the following is commonly used for providing the structural strength of truss bridges?

A) Rectangular units
B) Hexagonal units
C) Circular units
D) Triangular units

13

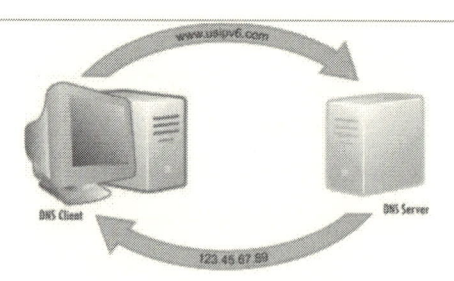

DNS (Domain Name System) is the Internet's system for converting alphabetic names into numeric addresses.

What is the role of a Domain Name System (DNS)?

A) It converts a domain name into a binary.
B) It translates a domain name into a hex.
C) It translates a domain name into an IP.
D) It changes a domain name into a URL.

14

Biotechnology includes the study and use of living organisms or cell processes to make or modify products.

The production of high-quality biofuel is a multistep industrial and biotechnological procedure. In the production of biofuel, the process of fermentation converts plant material into ethanol.

Which of the following about the production of biofuel is not correct?

A) Ethanol is a form of alcohol that can be produced by the fermentation of carbohydrates contained in plants.
B) The starch contained in the corn is broken down into glucose during the fermentation process.
C) Glucose is converted into ethanol and carbon dioxide with the action of yeast.
D) Ethanol is the biofuel, which is then mixed with gasoline in concentrations of 25 to 30 percent.

15

Which of the following areas of study are the key concepts of guidance, control, suspension, propulsion, and support taught in?

A) Biotechnical systems
B) Integrated systems
C) Transportation
D) Manufacturing

16

What is the other term for a computer's main memory?

A) Secondary storage
B) Primary storage
C) Auxiliary storage
D) Reserved storage

17

It is a type of **chart** that contains both bars and a line graph, where individual values are represented in descending order by bars, and the cumulative total is represented by the line.

Which of the following is explained above?

A) Bubble chart
B) Range chart
C) Pareto chart
D) Bar chart

18

Transportation is the movement of humans, animals, and goods from one location to another. Modes of transport include air, land (rail and road), water, cable, pipeline, and space.

Which of the following statements about transportation is not correct?

A) The world's first artificial satellite is Sputnik 1.
B) Skylab is the largest space station ever constructed.
C) A global positioning system (GPS) uses satellites to determine its location on earth.
D) The main transportation regulatory agency in the United States is The U.S. Department of Transportation.

19

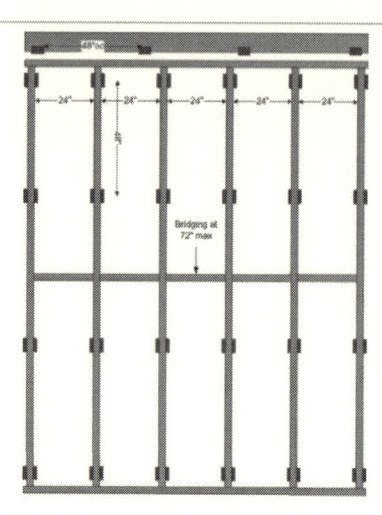

Which of the following is a horizontal structure used in framing to span an open space when constructing a house?

A) Headers
B) Sheeting
C) Joists
D) Footing

20

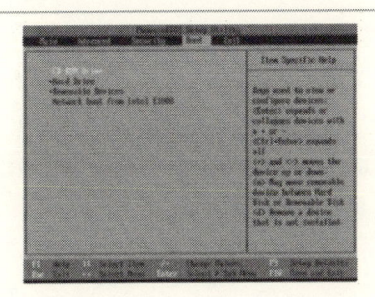

BIOS is a set of instructions that run to help load the operating system.

Which of the following is the operation of replacing the BIOS instructions stored on the ROM by a set of more efficient ones?

A) Flashing the BIOS
B) Changing the BIOS
C) Clearing the BIOS
D) Deleting the BIOS

21

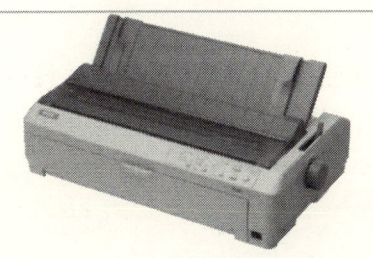

A printer is an external hardware output device that takes the electronic data stored on a computer or other device and generates a hard copy of it.

Which of the following printers are known to press characters or dots against an inked ribbon onto a paper through a mechanical head of retracting pins?

A) Ink-Jet
B) Dot-matrix
C) Thermal
D) Laser

22

Temperature changes affect the structural properties of metals. For example, higher temperatures increase the kinetic energy of electrons whereas lower temperatures decrease electron speed.

Which of the following materials is least affected by temperature changes?

A) Germanium
B) Silicon
C) Copper
D) Carbon

23

An instruction is an order given to a computer processor by a computer program.

Which of the following would allow users to interactively send instructions (such as printing and closing a window) to a computer using graphical icons?

A) GUI
B) Keyboard
C) Commands
D) Printer

24

There are some rules and conventions for communication between network devices. Networking computers use connecting devices and set up of strict regulations for communication to take place.

Which of the following refers to the rules and regulations of computer communication?

A) Internet
B) Protocols
C) Browser
D) Web

25

A file format is a structure of how information is stored in a computer file.

Which file format would be the most appropriate when data from a spreadsheet needs to be imported into a database package?

A) CSV (Comma Separated Values)
B) RTF (Rich Text Format)
C) HTML (Hypertext Markup Language)
D) PDF (Portable Document Format)

26

PPTP is an obsolete method for implementing virtual private networks, with many known security issues.

What does PPTP stand for?

A) Point to Point Transfer Protocol
B) Point to Point Traffic Protocol
C) Point to Point Tunneling Protocol
D) Point to Point Transmission Protocol

27

Volatile memory is computer storage that only maintains its data while the device is powered.

Which of the following can be classified as a volatile memory?

A) Cache
B) Hard Drive
C) Read-Only Memory (ROM)
D) Random-Access Memory (RAM)

28

Worm software mostly relies on security failures on the target computer to access it.

Which of the following best describes the malicious nature of worm software?

A) Sending data from a host computer to another unauthorized entity
B) Deleting or altering essential files stored on an infected computer
C) Self-replicating to spread across networks to other computers
D) Giving a remote hacker unauthorized access to a network computer

29

A word processor is an electronic device or computer software application, which performs the task of composing, editing, formatting, and printing of documents.

Which of the following is not a feature of a word processor?

A) Macros
B) Sending email
C) Borders and shading
D) Mail Merge and letter assistant

30

Materials-handling equipment is used across the stages of manufacturing and distributing to the disposal of products.

Which of the following guidance systems is mainly materials-handling?

A) Railroad
B) Escalator
C) Conveyor
D) Highway

31

Name and address book (NAB) is a book or a database used for storing entries called contacts.

Which of the following is the purpose of a name and address book in an email package?

A) Keeping the list of previously visited URL's
B) Keeping a list of all contacts and their email addresses
C) Attaching a file like a word document to a message
D) Attaching an email signature to an email

32

The cache is a space in your computer's hard drive and in RAM memory where your browser saves copies of previously visited Web pages.

Which of the following statements is true?

A) L2 cache is faster than L1 cache
B) A cache hit indicates that the information we are looking for is not in the cache
C) The Internet can also be used as a cache memory
D) There are several levels of cache in a computer

33

The engineering design process is also known as a series of steps that engineers follow to come up with a solution to a problem. Many times this solution involves designing a product (like a machine or computer code) that meets certain criteria and/or accomplishes a certain task.

Out of the options given below, which one is the last step in this process?

A) Creating solution
B) Testing and analysis
C) Generating idea
D) Improving the design

34

Computer software is supposed to have Internal Documentation if the notes on how and why various parts of code operate are included in the source code as comments.

Which of the following is the primary reason for producing internal program documentation?

A) Tracing the execution by printing output at critical branching points
B) Increasing program reliability by reporting and storing error codes
C) Providing explanations of code segments for maintenance and updates
D) Reducing execution time by improving memory allocation and usage

35

An internal modem is a network device on an expansion board that plugs into the motherboard.

By which of the following is an internal modem usually connected to a computer?

A) PCI Express slot
B) PCI slot
C) AGP slot
D) USB port

A motherboard is one of the essential parts of a computer system. It holds together many of the crucial components of a computer, including the central processing unit (CPU), memory and connectors for input and output devices.

Which of the following would indicate that the motherboard battery has failed?

A) Files on the hard disk are lost and corrupted.
B) Operating system passwords are lost.
C) Hardware settings, including virtual memory, revert to default values.
D) Hardware settings, including the current date and time, revert to default values.

SECTION 5 - TECHNOLOGY

#	Answer	Topic	Subtopic	#	Answer	Topic	Subtopic	#	Answer	Topic	Subtopic	#	Answer	Topic	Subtopic
1	C	TB	S3	10	B	TB	S2	19	C	TB	S2	28	C	TB	S1
2	B	TB	S2	11	A	TB	S3	20	A	TB	S1	29	D	TB	S1
3	A	TB	S1	12	D	TB	S2	21	B	TB	S1	30	B	TB	S2
4	C	TB	S3	13	C	TB	S1	22	C	TB	S2	31	B	TB	S1
5	B	TB	S2	14	D	TB	S4	23	A	TB	S1	32	D	TB	S1
6	A	TB	S3	15	C	TB	S2	24	B	TB	S1	33	D	TB	S2
7	D	TB	S2	16	B	TB	S1	25	A	TB	S1	34	C	TB	S1
8	A	TB	S3	17	C	TB	S2	26	C	TB	S1	35	B	TB	S1
9	A	TB	S2	18	B	TB	S3	27	D	TB	S1	36	D	TB	S1

Topics & Subtopics

Code	Description
SB1	Information & Communication Technologies
SB2	Manufacturing & Construction
SB3	Energy Power & Transportation

Code	Description
SB4	Biotechnology and Environmental Issues
TB	Technology

Made in United States
Orlando, FL
28 November 2023